2024 REFLECTIONS
2025 INTENTIONS

A New Year's journaling process to help you reflect, set intentions, and stay on track toward creating a life you love.

ALSO BY STEPHANIE MAY WILSON

Create A Life You Love

The Between Places

Every Single Moment

The Lipstick Gospel

The Lipstick Gospel Devotional

How to Make Friends in a New City

Love Your Single Life *Online Course*

Just Married *Online Course*

2024 REFLECTIONS
2025 INTENTIONS

STEPHANIE MAY WILSON

Copyright © 2024 by Stephanie May Wilson.
StephanieMayWilson.com
All rights reserved.

No part of this publication may be reproduced, stored in a retrieval system, or transmitted in any form or by any means, electronic, mechanical, photocopying, recording, scanning, or otherwise, without the prior written permission of the author, except in the case of brief quotations embodied in critical articles or reviews.

This publication is designed to provide accurate and authoritative information in regard to the subject matter covered. It is sold with the understanding that neither the author nor the publisher is engaged in rendering legal, investment, accounting or other professional services. While the publisher and author have used their best efforts in preparing this book, they make no representations or warranties with respect to the accuracy or completeness of the contents of this book and specifically disclaim any implied warranties of merchantability or fitness for a particular purpose. No warranty may be created or extended by sales representatives or written sales materials. The advice and strategies contained herein may not be suitable for your situation. You should consult with a professional when appropriate. Neither the publisher nor the author shall be liable for any loss of profit or any other commercial damages, including but not limited to special, incidental, consequential, personal, or other damages.

2024 Reflections, 2025 Intentions
A New Year's journaling process to help you reflect, set intentions,
and stay on track toward creating a life you love.
By Stephanie May Wilson

SELF HELP

ISBN: 978-1-7348715-3-1

Design by Carl Wilson
carlswilson.com

Printed in the United States of America

WELCOME

Hey friend,

Happy New Year! What a gift to get to spend this time with you!

Maybe we've been friends for a long time now. Perhaps you were around for the travel blog days, read *The Lipstick Gospel*, took my course, *Love Your Single Life*, and started listening to the *Girls Night Podcast* when I first started recording it from the floor of my bedroom closet.

But this might also be our first time meeting, so I wanted to take a quick second to introduce myself.

Hi, I'm Stephanie May Wilson (or just Steph now that we're friends!), and it's so great to meet you!

If we were sitting together in person, we'd be wearing comfy sweats, curled up on a couch in a beautiful place, and drinking either a cappuccino or champagne (since it is New Year's, after all!).

Currently, I'm sitting in a beautiful cafe in a 16th-century convent-turned-hotel, drinking a cappuccino and eating a chocolate croissant (and trying not to get it all over my laptop).

My family moved to Spain earlier this year, and this is one of my all-time favorite places to hang out, so I knew that this was where I wanted to sit when I wrote this guide.

For the last ten years, I've been living out my mission of "being who I needed when I was younger" to women who might be a step or two behind me in life — helping them navigate big decisions and life transitions.

That work culminated earlier this year when I released a brand new book, Create A Life You Love: How to quiet outside voices so you can finally hear your own, and gave a TEDx talk about it.

OH, and two months later, on our 10th wedding anniversary, my husband and I rented out our house, sold our cars (and most of our stuff), and packed up our twin three-year-olds to move to Spain. Casual, right?

People usually have one of two reactions to our big move: "That's awesome!" or "Are you crazy!" Either way, they want to know, "What made you decide to do that?"

There are about 10,000 reasons why we wanted to move our little family to Spain and chose to make this big move now. But the short story is that we're creating a life we love. And I'm on a mission to help you do the same—not create a life that looks like mine, but create a life that looks like you.

Through my books, courses, and podcast, Girls Night with Stephanie May Wilson, I've had the honor of mentoring more than a million women as they make decisions and navigate life transitions related to career, marriage, motherhood, and more.

With this new guide, I'm so excited to share a process with you that's helped me so much in creating a life I love. I do it every year as one year ends, and the next one begins, and now it's your turn.

You ready? Let's dive in!

All my love,

Steph

INTRODUCTION

NEW YEAR

I love the concept of New Year's Resolutions, don't you? The idea that you could finish a day with champagne and sparklers and a toast with your loved ones and wake up the next morning with all of your flaws and shortcomings miraculously gone? Yes, please!

The problem is that it rarely goes that way.

The statistics on New Year's Resolutions are at once conclusive and dismal. No matter what kind of resolutions we make or how we make them, they never seem to stick. Nobody follows through with them. But that never stopped me from trying.

I drank the 'New Year, New You' Kool-Aid for YEARS – buying into all the pressure to finish one year perfectly and begin the next on precisely the right foot.
My New Year's Eve plans had to be epic because, obviously, that one night was going to set the tone for the 365 days to follow. And then, no matter what happened on New Year's Eve (or how late I stayed out), I had to wake up bright and shiny first thing the next morning – bursting out of my hazy, "Why didn't I go to bed earlier" fog with a run and a green smoothie, ready to be my very best self.

MAKING PLANS

For years, I felt like the new year was my annual chance to completely reinvent myself – magically transform into the version I'd always wanted to be. So, sometime between Christmas and New Year's Eve, I'd sit down and make plans. My inner critic would pull out her red pen and attack me with it – circling all the ways I wasn't good enough so I could fix them, once and for all.

But instead of sparking the transformation I longed for, just a few weeks into January, I'd find myself more discouraged than ever — extra aware of all my flaws and more convinced than ever that I'd never get it together enough to correct them. (After all, I barely made it two weeks before falling short of everything I resolved to do!)

Finally, I realized that this whole thing — the pressure, the red pen, the anxiety, the feeling like a failure — was not the recipe for genuine life change — at least not for me. Also, it wasn't how I wanted to end one year and begin the next.

So, about ten years ago, I finally had enough. I threw out the idea of traditional New Year's Resolutions and came up with something different.

In an old notebook, I put together the New Year's reflection/goal-setting process I'd always been looking for — one that's thoughtful, intentional, dreamy, and full of warmth and kindness. I wrote a set of journaling prompts and brainstorming exercises to help me gracefully transition from one year to the next.

Ever since, this is what I have done: I take myself out to coffee with my journal and my favorite pen, and I ask and answer questions that help me reflect, reset, and dream for the year ahead — no resolutions in sight.

Now, don't get me wrong, I do start the year with some goals, things I want to do, and places I want to go. I'm a huge dreamer, and I also know that if we don't pick a destination or, at the very least, a direction we want to walk in, we could wander aimlessly forever.

Most people don't create a life they love by accident. It takes intentional effort. You have to pick a destination, chart a course, and make a plan.

And that's what we're here to do.

A YEAR FROM NOW, YOU'LL BE SO GLAD YOU STARTED TODAY

"I thought I'd be further along by now." Have you ever had that thought, or its almost identical cousin, "Why am I not making progress FASTER!?"?

I've had those thoughts about 1,000 times this year.

I have some big goals right now. They're not the kind you can knock out with a few weeks of work and dedication or by pulling an all-nighter, like a last-minute science fair project. They're the kind you have to buckle into for the long term. And there have been so many times this year where the progress has been so slow and truly imperceptible that I'm tempted to throw in the towel.

But every time I get close, there's the same reminder waiting for me:

START EARLY, DON'T QUIT, GIVE IT TIME TO GROW

This reminder has taken several forms throughout the year, and one of my favorites came from the trees in our neighborhood.

Once we officially decided to uproot our lives in Nashville and move to Spain, our next step was to rent out our house. We wanted to get it rented out early—just in case the process was harder or more complicated than anticipated. So, a little over a year ago, we found renters for our house, packed up all of our belongings, and moved to a rental home.

Between our deeply rooted Nashville life and our wild adventure to Spain, we had a year-long layover in a recently built suburb 30 minutes north of the city.

The neighborhood is large and full of new houses, which have been built slowly over the last six or seven years.

Pulling into the neighborhood, you're greeted by a canopy of large, leafy trees. They're beautiful and perfectly line the streets.

But as you continue through the neighborhood and into the sections in the back that are still under construction, the trees are much smaller. Finally, you end up on the street where our rental house was, with a tree in the front yard that would make Charley Brown's Christmas tree look impressive.

There are no big, leafy, established trees in sight.

I'd drive through the covering of trees every day, and every day, I'd be reminded that the only difference between the twig in our front yard and the beautiful trees at the entrance was time.

The trees at the entrance had been there longer. They had been planted years earlier, so they'd had time to grow.

I came across a Chinese Proverb this year that reflects this perfectly.

It says, "The best time to plant a tree was 20 years ago. The second best time is now."

PLANT WHAT YOU WANT TO GROW

When we first moved to Nashville, I was walking around my favorite park, where I always did my very best thinking. That day, I was taking an inventory of my life: how's it going? What's going well? What would I like to see change? As I did, some flowers next to the trail caught my eye.

Now — I have to stop here and tell you that the analogy I'm about to share would be WAY better if I were one of those girls with a beautiful garden. Unfortunately, I am not that girl. I've killed everything I've ever tried to grow.

But seeing those flowers reminded me of the only thing I know to be true about gardening: If you want something to grow, you have to plant a seed. If you want a particular thing to grow, you need to plant that kind of seed. The kind of seed you plant dictates what kind of plant will grow—and that's true every time!

If you want a tomato plant to grow, you need to plant tomato seeds. That's just the way it works. In fact, it's the only way it works.

If you don't plant a seed, nothing will grow. And if you plant a bell pepper seed, you won't get a pumpkin. That seed will never produce the kind of fruit you're looking for.

As I continued walking, I realized this is true of our lives, too.

The seeds we plant in our lives turn into something, so if we want something specific to exist in our lives, we have to plant those seeds.

This is true of how we take care of our bodies, our relationships with friends, our careers, the goals we want to achieve, and how we spend our money.

If we spend money without thinking, we won't get out of debt. If we constantly cancel plans, say 'no' to invitations, and spend our evenings at home binging Netflix, we're not going to have the deep, connected group of friends we've been longing for.

We have to plant the seeds we want to grow.

But here's the problem. If you're anything like me, you have the planting part down. Plant a seed? No problem! In the beginning, you're all confidence and good intentions. But shortly after that seed hits the dirt, you're crushed by a wave of discouragement when a fully formed and fruited plant doesn't immediately shoot out of the ground.

(What do you mean these five crunches didn't immediately turn into a six-pack!?)

Apparently, it just doesn't happen that fast — not with most truly worthwhile goals. Good things take time, care, and consistency.

A few months ago, still hard at work learning this lesson, I came across a quote from the habit master himself, James Clear.

He says,

"If you get one percent better each day for one year, you'll end up thirty-seven times better by the time you're done."

That's SO compelling to me. I can't get 1000% better overnight — no matter how much I may want to. But I can get 1% better. And I can't stop thinking about the fact that those improvements compound over time — a snowball rolling down the hill and gaining momentum as it grows.

WHAT DOES THIS MEAN FOR THE NEW YEAR?

Okay, so if you add all of these ideas together, here's what I've come up with:

If you want something to exist in your life, you have to grow that thing. Growth takes time, so the sooner you get that seed in the ground, the better. That seed CAN'T start growing until you plant it.

And then, little by little, day by day, 1% at a time, you tend that seed. You give it water, sunlight, attention, and care.

The progress might feel slow (and at times, completely stalled!), but if you keep doing a little bit each day, you'll wake up a year from now and see that your little seed and your daily acts of faithfulness have turned into something beautiful — and over time, that growth will gain more momentum.

Even though we no longer live there, I still think about the trees in our old neighborhood almost daily. I wonder how much bigger our little tree is than the last time I saw it, and I remember that just like that little tree is growing a little bit each day, so am I.

"A YEAR FROM NOW, YOU'LL BE SO GLAD YOU STARTED TODAY."

SMW

2024 REFLECTIONS | 2025 INTENTIONS

THESE IDEAS WILL BE OUR GUIDE THROUGHOUT THIS PROCESS

So today, as we finish one year and begin another, these ideas will guide us. This guided journal will help you take the pause a fresh calendar affords us all and reflect on where you were a year ago, what you planted, what you've tended, and what fruit you're living with today as a result.

You'll zoom out to see the progress, growth, and big leaps that all those little (sometimes seemingly insignificant!) steps accomplished.

Maybe as you look back at 2024, you see some things you wanted to happen in your life this year, but you simply didn't plant the seed. Or maybe you did what I'm so guilty of doing – you planted the seed, looked for magic, overnight Jack-And-The-Beanstalk type growth, and got discouraged when you didn't see it, so you threw in the towel.

Or maybe you see that while you wanted friendship or health or spiritual growth to happen in your life this last year, you were planting canceled plans, too much time scrolling social media, and a zillion hours on your laptop instead of tending to your health. With a little distance, you can see that the seeds you were planting were never going to grow into the fruit you were hoping for.

So then, the second half of this book is a chance to do things differently in 2025.

GRACE UPON GRACE

But throughout this whole process – whether you're reflecting on this last year or setting your course for the next one – I want you to do it with grace for yourself.

You had a big year, my friend. Whatever this year contained, I'm 10000% sure that parts were beautiful and other parts were hard.

No matter what you went through this year personally, this was a challenging year to be a human collectively. We've had a lot of those lately.

So, as you approach this time of reflection, I'll help you make sure you're doing so with a hug for all that you did, all you tried to do, and all you didn't do because of all you had to go through.

Red pen and self-condemnation are not welcome at this New Year's party!

Before we officially get started, let's talk details.

HOW TO USE THIS BOOK

WHEN TO DO THIS BOOK

There's nothing magically transformative about the beginning of a New Year. It carries as much weight as you put on it. Also, a fresh start is available to you whenever you need one. With that in mind, I would prefer to start the new year around January 5th. I'm just not ready on January 1st. I never have been.

When you work through this journal is up to you.

If you want to do it in that beautiful, twinkly lull between Christmas and New Year's, do it then. If you're up early on January 1st with a coffee, a green smoothie, and a fire in your belly to be a new you in this new year, then by all means, do it then!

But if you're like me and need to reschedule the new year until the holidays are over and you're back home, unpacked, ready to dive into real life again, feel free to do that.

My new year will start around January 9th this year, and that's perfect for me right now.

HOW LONG WILL IT TAKE TO USE THE BOOK

The short answer is that you can spend as much or as little time working through this as you want to. It's totally up to you, of course!

But if you're looking for a guideline, see if you can give yourself at least three uninterrupted hours: 90 minutes to reflect on the year that's coming to a close and 90 minutes to look ahead toward the new year.

Where to do this book:
If you can, do this workbook alone. Go someplace you enjoy, someplace you can unwind, someplace you're not going to be interrupted, someplace you can think.

That can be a coffee shop, in your bedroom, under the Christmas tree, or at your desk, wherever you feel comfortable, safe, and inspired.

HOW TO DO THIS BOOK

In my experience, there are two kinds of people in the world: bakers and cooks.

Bakers are the rule-followers among us, the ones who appreciate order and thoroughness, who want to get the absolute most out of an experience and appreciate a recipe to keep them on track.

The cooks are more go-with-the-flow. They follow their nose, gut, and whatever they can find in the fridge. They don't need a recipe, and frankly, they often don't want one. They want to do things their own way with their own flair in the way that feels right to them.

Both are more than welcome here!

Throughout this workbook, I will give you specific instructions—just in case you are more of a baker. But if you're a cook, feel free to toss out my instructions and make your own rules. This process, this time, it's yours. I'll walk you through it step-by-step if that's helpful for you. But if it's not, feel free to do whatever works for you.

So, are you ready?

Pour your favorite beverage, cozy into somewhere comfy, pull out your favorite pen, and start by reflecting on 2024.

2024 REFLECTIONS

WARM UP QUESTIONS

Spend about five minutes answering the following questions to get your wheels turning and your heart into a reflective posture. There are no right or wrong answers. Just write down the first things that come to mind:

If I had to describe 2024 in one word, it would be _____.

2024 was a year full of _____, and _____, and _____.

Five wonderful things that happened this year:

_____
_____
_____
_____
_____

Five tough things that happened this year:

_____
_____
_____
_____
_____

2024 REFLECTIONS | 2025 INTENTIONS

A lesson I learned in 2024 that I want to make sure to take with me into the future is...

_____
_____
_____
_____
_____

WHERE WERE YOU A YEAR AGO?

A year is a long time. So much can (and usually does!) happen in a year, so the idea of reflecting on it all at once might leave you with a major case of writer's block.

I've divided life into eight categories to make this a little bit easier.

The eight categories are:

- Mental & Physical Health
- Faith & Spirituality
- Family
- Friends
- Romantic Relationships
- Finances
- Work
- Enjoying Your Life

For each of these categories, I will ask you four different questions.

The four questions are:

- How were things going in this area of your life a year ago?
- What seeds did you plant this year?
- How did you water those seeds?
- How are things going in this area of your life today?

These questions will help you think through what's changed in your life this year, how you've grown, what you've been working on, and really, track your progress and see how much bigger your tree is today than it was a year ago. (To continue with our arboreal metaphor!)

As I said, you can approach this as a baker or a cook. If you want to answer all of the prompts, you can. If some don't feel particularly applicable, feel free to skip them! I also included a few blank sections at the end so you can add any categories I might have left out.

ONE THING TO NOTE

As you go through these questions, you'll likely come to several — or even several categories — where you don't have much to report. My physical health (eating enough vegetables and doing intentional exercise) would have been graded a C- at the beginning of this year. And you know what? At the end of the year, it's not much different. My physical health took a bit of a backseat this year. But that will be the case for all of us in various areas of life.

Significant growth in one area requires you to be in maintenance mode in others. We only have so much time, energy, and resources to give.

So know that if you go through this and realize, "I made a ton of progress with my finances this year but not much with making friends" — that's not something to be ashamed of. You didn't do anything wrong. You allocated your limited time and energy where you thought was best. But if you want to do that differently in the coming year, you absolutely can.

MENTAL & PHYSICAL HEALTH

How were things going in this area of your life a year ago?

2024 REFLECTIONS | 2025 INTENTIONS

MENTAL & PHYSICAL HEALTH

What seeds did you plant this year?

2024 REFLECTIONS | 2025 INTENTIONS

MENTAL & PHYSICAL HEALTH

How did you water those seeds?

2024 REFLECTIONS | 2025 INTENTIONS

MENTAL & PHYSICAL HEALTH

How are things going in this area of your life today?

2024 REFLECTIONS | 2025 INTENTIONS

WORK

How were things going in this area of your life a year ago?

2024 REFLECTIONS | 2025 INTENTIONS

WORK

What seeds did you plant this year?

2024 REFLECTIONS | 2025 INTENTIONS

WORK

How did you water those seeds?

2024 REFLECTIONS | 2025 INTENTIONS

WORK

How are things going in this area of your life today?

2024 REFLECTIONS | 2025 INTENTIONS

FINANCES

How were things going in this area of your life a year ago?

2024 REFLECTIONS | 2025 INTENTIONS

FINANCES

What seeds did you plant this year?

2024 REFLECTIONS | 2025 INTENTIONS

FINANCES

How did you water those seeds?

2024 REFLECTIONS | 2025 INTENTIONS

FINANCES

How are things going in this area of your life today?

2024 REFLECTIONS | 2025 INTENTIONS

FAMILY

How were things going in this area of your life a year ago?

2024 REFLECTIONS | 2025 INTENTIONS

FAMILY

What seeds did you plant this year?

2024 REFLECTIONS | 2025 INTENTIONS

FAMILY

How did you water those seeds?

2024 REFLECTIONS | 2025 INTENTIONS

FAMILY

How are things going in this area of your life today?

2024 REFLECTIONS | 2025 INTENTIONS

ROMANTIC RELATIONSHIPS

How were things going in this area of your life a year ago?

2024 REFLECTIONS | 2025 INTENTIONS

ROMANTIC RELATIONSHIPS

What seeds did you plant this year?

2024 REFLECTIONS | 2025 INTENTIONS

ROMANTIC RELATIONSHIPS

How did you water those seeds?

2024 REFLECTIONS | 2025 INTENTIONS

ROMANTIC RELATIONSHIPS

How are things going in this area of your life today?

2024 REFLECTIONS | 2025 INTENTIONS

FAITH & SPIRITUALITY

How were things going in this area of your life a year ago?

2024 REFLECTIONS | 2025 INTENTIONS

FAITH & SPIRITUALITY

What seeds did you plant this year?

2024 REFLECTIONS | 2025 INTENTIONS

FAITH & SPIRITUALITY

How did you water those seeds?

2024 REFLECTIONS | 2025 INTENTIONS

FAITH & SPIRITUALITY

How are things going in this area of your life today?

2024 REFLECTIONS | 2025 INTENTIONS

(These blanks are for you to write in your own categories!)

How were things going in this area of your life a year ago?

2024 REFLECTIONS | 2025 INTENTIONS

What seeds did you plant this year?

2024 REFLECTIONS | 2025 INTENTIONS

How did you water those seeds?

2024 REFLECTIONS | 2025 INTENTIONS

How are things going in this area of your life today?

2024 REFLECTIONS | 2025 INTENTIONS

_____
(These blanks are for you to write in your own categories!)

How were things going in this area of your life a year ago?

2024 REFLECTIONS | 2025 INTENTIONS

What seeds did you plant this year?

2024 REFLECTIONS | 2025 INTENTIONS

How did you water those seeds?

2024 REFLECTIONS | 2025 INTENTIONS

How are things going in this area of your life today?

2024 REFLECTIONS | 2025 INTENTIONS

_____

(These blanks are for you to write in your own categories!)

How were things going in this area of your life a year ago?

2024 REFLECTIONS | 2025 INTENTIONS

What seeds did you plant this year?

2024 REFLECTIONS | 2025 INTENTIONS

How did you water those seeds?

2024 REFLECTIONS | 2025 INTENTIONS

How are things going in this area of your life today?

2024 REFLECTIONS | 2025 INTENTIONS

2025 INTENTIONS

WARM UP QUESTIONS

There are two ladies in my life I think about a lot—the 6-year-old girl I used to be and the 86-year-old woman I hope to be one day.

It's so easy to get caught up in what other people think. (How's that for the understatement of the year?) There are about a gagillion things you could do this year, ways you could grow, resolutions you could make, and standards you could hold yourself to.

Most of them are fine, and many are even good. But you can't do all of them, and if you try, you'll miss out on the things most important to you. There's just not enough time to focus on everything.

That's why I like to consult my six and 86-year-old selves. I love having them weigh in.

My 6-year-old self was fearless and overflowing with passion – she had all the innocence and confidence that comes with life before self-consciousness enters the chat. She was just starting to figure out what it meant to be passionate about something. She was just getting her first taste of what it felt like to create. At age six, I wrote my first book on computer paper that my first-grade teacher folded in half and stapled at the seam. I could have written a hundred of them; I loved it so much.

I love thinking about my six-year-old self because that's when some of the core pieces of who I am started to peek out, and none of them had had a chance to be whack-a-moled yet. (Womp womp, looking at you, middle school!).

And then there's my 86-year-old self. I don't know who she'll be yet, of course, but I'm hoping she'll be a lot like my grandmother, Anne.

My Gramie, Anne, is one of the most important people I've had in my life. (We named our daughter Annie after her!). Anne had a lot in common with my 6-year-old self, actually. She was fearless. She was funny. She was vibrant, independent, and a rule-breaker in the best ways.

I spent as much time with her as I possibly could in the 28 years I had her in my life, and when I think about my 86-year-old self, I try to imagine what Gramie Anne would have to say about these things.

So to get your wheels turning about the immediate future, let's spend a second imagining what your past and far-off future selves would want that to look like:

If my 6-year-old self had her way, in 2025, my life would include more:

_____
_____
_____
_____

If my 6-year-old self had her way, in 2025, my life would include less:

_____
_____
_____
_____

If my 86-year-old self had her way, in 2025, my life would include more:

_____
_____
_____
_____

If my 86-year-old self had her way, in 2025, my life would include less:

_____
_____
_____
_____

WHAT'S THE BEST THAT COULD HAPPEN?

In just a minute, you'll write down some concrete dreams and plans for 2025 —but we have one more stop before we get there.

Sometimes, after a hard year or a stretch of hard years, our dreams stop being audacious or even true to what we actually want, and they end up looking something like this,

"I just want things to get a tiny bit better."

"If we could just stop trending in the wrong direction and level out, I'd be really grateful for that."

"I just hope things don't get worse."

Yes, yes to all of those things. Yes to things getting a little bit better and to downward trends changing direction. But I think when we spend so much time discouraged and sitting in this "Ugh, just please don't get worse" kind of place, we lose the vision of where we're going.

We start living in "What's the worst that can happen?" and forget all about the flip side – "What's the best that could happen?"

I get caught up in this type of thinking every so often, so today, as we're beginning a whole new year, I want to invite you into one more exercise. I've never done this exercise before, but I wanted to this year, and I thought it could be fun to do it together.

WHAT'S THE BEST THAT COULD HAPPEN?

On the lines below, pick a category, a part of your life, something you're working on, or something you've been hoping for. Then, in the space below that line, brainstorm: What is the best thing that could happen in this area of your life? What's the coolest thing that could happen, the most miraculous thing, the most amazing thing, what's the most unbelievably awesome thing that could happen? Let yourself get lost in it for a while. Think as big as you can and be specific about the things you're writing down.

We don't have to default to the worst that can happen—wonderful things can happen, too

2024 REFLECTIONS | 2025 INTENTIONS

In this area of my life _____ what's the best that can happen?

_____
_____
_____
_____
_____
_____
_____
_____
_____
_____

In this area of my life _____ what's the best that can happen?

_____
_____
_____
_____
_____
_____
_____
_____
_____
_____

2024 REFLECTIONS | 2025 INTENTIONS

In this area of my life _____ what's the best that can happen?

In this area of my life _____ what's the best that can happen?

2024 REFLECTIONS | 2025 INTENTIONS

In this area of my life _____ what's the best that can happen?

___

In this area of my life _____ what's the best that can happen?

2024 REFLECTIONS | 2025 INTENTIONS

In this area of my life _____ what's the best that can happen?

___
___
___
___
___
___
___
___
___
___
___
___

In this area of my life _____ what's the best that can happen?

___
___
___
___
___
___
___
___
___
___
___
___

WHERE DO YOU WANT TO BE A YEAR FROM NOW?

Okay, now that you've looked at your life from different perspectives and now that you've reminded yourself to look for the best that can happen (instead of just defaulting to the worst!), it's time to make some plans:

Similarly to how we did when reflecting on 2024, in several of the most important areas of your life, you'll have a chance to look ahead —imagining where you might want to be this time a year from now and what you need to put into place today and over the next year to make those hopes and dreams a reality.

Remember that there's no right way to do this. While many people will tell you precisely what you should want your life to look like, the truth is that your direction is up to you.

After all, you're the only one who truly has to walk in it and who has to live with the consequences of your choices.

I've spent the last two years writing a book for women who are making big decisions about their lives. Here's a little snippet that captures the heart of it perfectly.

"Here's a hard truth. Just because people have strong opinions about the right way to live a life doesn't mean they're right. It doesn't mean their way is the only way, and it doesn't mean it's the only way (or the right way) for you.

There's no one right way to build a life. A beautiful life isn't one-size-fits-all. It can't possibly be. Everyone is different.

So instead of trying to figure out who the world wants us to be and how we can squeeze, shove, and contort ourselves into that exact mold, let's figure out who we are, what makes us us, and then be the people we are with our whole heart.

Instead of building a life that some people will think is amazing and other people will think falls hopelessly short, let's spend our time building a life we actually want to live. A life we feel at home in."

- Create A Life You Love: How to quiet outside voices so you can finally hear your own

YOU GET TO DECIDE

Those words have changed everything for me. They've given me agency over my life in a way I'd never experienced before and taught me how to hear and honor my own voice!

Of course, making massive decisions about your life is easier said than done, and that's why I love my New Year's reflection and intention tradition so much.

Author Annie Dillard says, "How we spend our days is, of course, how we spend our lives."

That's true with our years as well.

Our lives are a stack of the years they contain. And so sometimes, instead of deciding on a big-picture direction for our lives, it's easier to concentrate on what it looks like to take a year-long step forward. Or maybe you know exactly where you want to go, but that dream is so big and overwhelming that it's hard to imagine how you'll achieve it.

How you'll achieve it is one day, one week, one month, one year at a time.

This year is a piece of the puzzle, a block in the big stack that makes up your life story. How you live it matters, so for the 90 minutes or so, you'll have the space to start thinking through what you want that to look like. What do you want to spend this beautiful, precious year of your life doing? And as you're sitting down a year from now to reflect on 2025, what do you want your life to look like on that day?

MENTAL & PHYSICAL HEALTH

What do you want things to look like a year from now in this area of your life?

_____
_____
_____
_____
_____
_____
_____
_____
_____
_____
_____
_____
_____
_____
_____
_____
_____
_____
_____
_____
_____
_____
_____
_____

2024 REFLECTIONS | 2025 INTENTIONS

MENTAL & PHYSICAL HEALTH

What seeds do you need to plant to make that possible?

2024 REFLECTIONS | 2025 INTENTIONS

MENTAL & PHYSICAL HEALTH

When and how are you going to plant those seeds?

2024 REFLECTIONS | 2025 INTENTIONS

MENTAL & PHYSICAL HEALTH

What small, consistent ways will you tend those seeds to help them grow?

2024 REFLECTIONS | 2025 INTENTIONS

WORK

What do you want things to look like a year from now in this area of your life?

2024 REFLECTIONS | 2025 INTENTIONS

WORK

What seeds do you need to plant to make that possible?

2024 REFLECTIONS | 2025 INTENTIONS

WORK

When and how are you going to plant those seeds?

2024 REFLECTIONS | 2025 INTENTIONS

WORK

What small, consistent ways will you tend those seeds to help them grow?

2024 REFLECTIONS | 2025 INTENTIONS

FINANCES

What do you want things to look like a year from now in this area of your life?

2024 REFLECTIONS | 2025 INTENTIONS

FINANCES

What seeds do you need to plant to make that possible?

2024 REFLECTIONS | 2025 INTENTIONS

FINANCES

When and how are you going to plant those seeds?

2024 REFLECTIONS | 2025 INTENTIONS

FINANCES

What small, consistent ways will you tend those seeds to help them grow?

2024 REFLECTIONS | 2025 INTENTIONS

FAMILY

What do you want things to look like a year from now in this area of your life?

2024 REFLECTIONS | 2025 INTENTIONS

FAMILY

What seeds do you need to plant to make that possible?

2024 REFLECTIONS | 2025 INTENTIONS

FAMILY

When and how are you going to plant those seeds?

2024 REFLECTIONS | 2025 INTENTIONS

FAMILY

What small, consistent ways will you tend those seeds to help them grow?

2024 REFLECTIONS | 2025 INTENTIONS

ROMANTIC RELATIONSHIPS

What do you want things to look like a year from now in this area of your life?

2024 REFLECTIONS | 2025 INTENTIONS

ROMANTIC RELATIONSHIPS

What seeds do you need to plant to make that possible?

2024 REFLECTIONS | 2025 INTENTIONS

ROMANTIC RELATIONSHIPS

When and how are you going to plant those seeds?

2024 REFLECTIONS | 2025 INTENTIONS

ROMANTIC RELATIONSHIPS

What small, consistent ways will you tend those seeds to help them grow?

2024 REFLECTIONS | 2025 INTENTIONS

FAITH & SPIRITUALITY

What do you want things to look like a year from now in this area of your life?

2024 REFLECTIONS | 2025 INTENTIONS

FAITH & SPIRITUALITY

What seeds do you need to plant to make that possible?

2024 REFLECTIONS | 2025 INTENTIONS

FAITH & SPIRITUALITY

When and how are you going to plant those seeds?

2024 REFLECTIONS | 2025 INTENTIONS

FAITH & SPIRITUALITY

What small, consistent ways will you tend those seeds to help them grow?

2024 REFLECTIONS | 2025 INTENTIONS

_____
(These blanks are for you to write in your own categories!)

What do you want things to look like a year from now in this area of your life?

2024 REFLECTIONS | 2025 INTENTIONS

What seeds do you need to plant to make that possible?

2024 REFLECTIONS | 2025 INTENTIONS

When and how are you going to plant those seeds?

2024 REFLECTIONS | 2025 INTENTIONS

_____

What small, consistent ways will you tend those seeds to help them grow?

2024 REFLECTIONS | 2025 INTENTIONS

_____
(These blanks are for you to write in your own categories!)

What do you want things to look like a year from now in this area of your life?

2024 REFLECTIONS | 2025 INTENTIONS

_____

What seeds do you need to plant to make that possible?

2024 REFLECTIONS | 2025 INTENTIONS

When and how are you going to plant those seeds?

2024 REFLECTIONS | 2025 INTENTIONS

What small, consistent ways will you tend those seeds to help them grow?

2024 REFLECTIONS | 2025 INTENTIONS

_____

(These blanks are for you to write in your own categories!)

What do you want things to look like a year from now in this area of your life?

2024 REFLECTIONS | 2025 INTENTIONS

What seeds do you need to plant to make that possible?

2024 REFLECTIONS | 2025 INTENTIONS

When and how are you going to plant those seeds?

2024 REFLECTIONS | 2025 INTENTIONS

What small, consistent ways will you tend those seeds to help them grow?

2024 REFLECTIONS | 2025 INTENTIONS

LAST STOP

Now, with a little more color in your cheeks, hope in your heart, and a plan for moving forward, this is where we'll finish up.

I've included three options for ending this process — you can do all of them, or feel free to pick and choose if one feels like a better fit.

The first is a prayer for the year (with two options for how to pray it), and the second is a letter of encouragement for yourself as you start this new year.

PRAYERS FOR 2025

Of all the elements of faith, prayer comes the most naturally to me. Returning to our analogy about cooking and baking, I'm a total cook when it comes to prayer. I can riff, throw all kinds of words together, and pray in public; it doesn't feel awkward or intimidating to me. But because I can string so many words together so quickly, sometimes I forget to watch for what God does with the prayers once I pray them.

Because of that, one of the most powerful prayer exercises I've ever done is to write one prayer and repeat it daily for a long time.

Shortly after college, when I was traveling around the world for a year, a pastor in Romania gave me a written prayer that I just loved. It perfectly captured the things I wanted to happen in me, my life, and the world. And so every day, when I woke up in the morning, I read it out loud—word for word. Something profound shifted in me that year through that daily practice.

A few years later, my family had some things going on, and some big things were happening in my friends' lives, too. There was a long list of ways that my people and I needed God to show up for us, and I wanted to see what He would do if —instead of showing up every day with a word salad — I showed up every day and asked for the exact same thing.

It's not that I thought God would answer one prayer and wouldn't answer the other — it's more that I wanted to be more disciplined in my prayers and more diligent about looking for how God was answering them.

So that's what I did. I wrote down a list of prayer requests and read them out loud every day for a year. Then, I wrote down the date that each prayer was answered.

This powerful process brought me so much peace, so I'm glad to share it with you.

So, in the space below, I invite you to do one of those things if you'd like to. You can write out a word-for-word prayer that you want to read regularly — or write out a list of things you want to pray for consistently this year. If you do the latter, I will leave you some space so you can record when you see those prayers answered. It's really such a powerful practice.

2025 PRAYER

2024 REFLECTIONS | 2025 INTENTIONS

PRAYERS

ANSWERS

LOVE LETTER FOR THE YEAR AHEAD

Here's our very last stop: A love letter from you to you as you walk into this new year.

When we think about our most important relationships, one that rarely makes the list is the relationship we have with ourselves. It's a little bit mind-bending to think about it this way, but you are the most consistent companion you'll ever have. The voice you hear the most, the words you listen to the most—they don't come from anyone else; they come from you.

And that's why how we treat ourselves matters so much. It's almost impossible to do anything in life if the inner critic in your head is constantly screaming that you're not good enough.

A letter of encouragement is a step in the opposite direction—a step toward being on your own team—something that's profoundly powerful and beautiful but also difficult to do.

So, last but not least, write yourself a pep talk, a note of encouragement and love for this upcoming year.

Practice being on your own team and tell yourself the things you know you need to hear to take on this next year the way you want to.

LOVE LETTER FOR THE YEAR AHEAD

Date: _____   Current Location: _____

2024 REFLECTIONS | 2025 INTENTIONS

2024 REFLECTIONS | 2025 INTENTIONS

Friend, you did it!

You carved out some time to be thoughtful and reflective, to dream, and to decide on the direction you want to walk in this next year. That in itself is such an achievement. As we finish, I want to return to the last words I shared in my book, Create A Life You Love, because they fit perfectly here, too.

"There's not one right way to build a life. You get to decide. You get to figure out who you are, what makes you you and then be you with your whole heart — building a life you're excited about and proud of, a life that's a beautiful reflection of the woman who chose it, a life that looks and feels like you.

And when we do this, not only are we creating a life we love — a life that's creative and authentic and free — we're also paving the way for other women to do the same. We're showing our little sisters, our nieces, our daughters, and our granddaughters who a woman can be and what a woman can do. We're showing them that girls can do anything (but don't have to do everything, thank goodness!). We're opening up a world of possibilities in a kaleidoscope of different colors.

You're brave, and strong, and good, and worthy of a life you love. And I'm cheering you on every step of the way as you pursue exactly that."

All my love,

Stephanie May Wilson

ABOUT THE AUTHOR

Author, top podcaster, and TEDx speaker Stephanie May Wilson is on a mission to be who she needed when she was younger - -walking women through life's biggest decisions and transitions. Through her books, podcast, and online courses, Stephanie helps women take the pressure off of what their lives are "supposed" to look like, figure out where they actually want to go in life, and take the steps to get there.

Stephanie has been featured on NBC, ABC, CBS, and the Anthropologie blog. She has also been a longtime blog contributor for CNBC's Nightly Business Report, Darling magazine, and the Christian Mingle blog.

When she's not writing, speaking, or recording a podcast episode, Stephanie is usually packing for an adventure with her husband, Carl, laughing with her close tribe of girlfriends, or curled up in her new home in Spain with her twin toddlers, Annie and Quinn.

CREATE A LIFE YOU LOVE

Introducing my newest book, *Create a Life You Love:*
How to Quiet Outside Voices So You Can Finally Hear Your Own

Create a Life You Love is for the woman who...

- Isn't where she thought she'd be by this point in her life.
- Is making a massive decision — she's swimming in pro & con lists, but she still has no idea what to do.
- Knows exactly what she wants, she just can't seem to actually get it.
- Has no clue what she wants — but knows she doesn't want what she's supposed to want, and feels consumed by the conflict raging inside her.
- Is juggling several dreams — feeling like she's playing Tetris with her hopes, dreams, body, finances, and most important relationships — and she's wondering how (and if!) it'll all fit together!

Create a Life You Love is a guided journey of self-discovery, helping you take the pressure off what you think your life is supposed to look like by now and intentionally, confidently, and authentically build the life you actually want to live — a life that looks and feels like YOU.

Head to StephanieMayWilson.com/create to order your copy today!

Made in United States
Troutdale, OR
12/15/2024

26622681R00117